FAITH AND SCIENCE

A Journey into God's Mystical Love

TEACHER'S GUIDE

Robert J. Hesse, Ph.D.

Reflections by Jan Masterson

ROYALTY DONATONS – 100% of author royalties are donated to non-profit 501(C)(3), Contemplative Network (www.contemplative.net), formed in 2011 to teach interfaith contemplative prayer, sponsor scientific research on its healing effects, and establish ministries based on the research.

The Crossroad Publishing Company
1 Blue Hill Plaza Lobby Level, Suite 1509
Pearl River, New York 10965

ISBN: 9780824589028

Front Cover by Author
Editing by Jan Masterson

Cover Photo: Penguins, Half Moon Island, Antarctic - Photo

REVIEWS

STUDENT REVIEWS OF THE TEACHER'S GUIDE FOR

FAITH AND SCIENCE: A JOURNEY INTO GOD'S MYSTICAL LOVE

SPRING 2023 GRADUATE COURSE AT

THE UNIVERSITY OF ST. THOMAS

HOUSTON, TEXAS

"The *Teacher's Guide* accompanying Dr. Robert Hesse's text *Faith & Science* offers both teachers and students rich and detailed support in reframing and processing the content of each chapter. Ultimately, the guide helps clarify not only an understanding of the course's objectives, but also one's personal response to the synergy that arises from both faith and science concerning the universe, humanity and God."

Janice Reed

≈≈≈≈≈≈≈≈≈≈≈≈≈≈≈

"I read "Faith and Science, A Journey Into God's Mystical Love" by Robert Hesse and later attended a course on his book by the same name at the University of St Thomas in Houston Texas taught by Dr. Hesse. Both were deeply enriching experiences. I recently received the *Faith and Science Teachers Guide*. Although I am not a teacher, I find this highly recommended guide to be excellent in providing a concise, in-depth approach to offering guidance to anyone wanting to explore Dr. Hesse's book in more depth."

Bill Gorsky

≈≈≈≈≈≈≈≈≈≈≈≈≈≈≈

"The Book "Faith and Science" by Dr. Robert J. Hesse is a thought-provoking book which bridges the gap between faith and science and it brings perspective and harmony on how they both intersect and converge. Dr. Hesse uses his lifelong love and understanding of both faith and science and fuses them in a simplistic way merging these scientific principles and religious doctrines into a relationship and creates an accessible way of incorporating ease of understanding for all.

Dr. Hesse's *Teaching Guide* is a road map to seek further explanation in reconciling one's understanding and offers an opportunity for all to share in this teaching through the support of this book. With humility and open mindedness, all can come to know God's great awe!"

Susan Dewlen

≈≈≈≈≈≈≈≈≈≈≈≈≈≈

"Thank you, Dr Hesse, for the great material covered in class, so far it has been the most exciting class I have taken, I will reread the book in the summer and revisit the recording of the classes. God bless."

Sol Labanca

≈≈≈≈≈≈≈≈≈≈≈≈≈≈

"Faith & Science as a course was nothing I could have predicted - from day one, it took me on a journey that was better than fiction because it led me into deep contemplation via a seasoned veteran of both topics. I found myself touting the miracle that God once again is greater than I can imagine, yet this time it was not at all dogmatic. Instead, it reframed my view on all creation, and for that, I am grateful."

Sarah Ellison Lewis

≈≈≈≈≈≈≈≈≈≈≈≈≈≈

"As a student in Dr. Hesse's first class about this book, I was very unexpectedly taken on a journey of our magnificent God-created universe simultaneously into myself at a subatomic level. This is a personal book written by a man struggling to comprehend the relationship of our spirituality deep within us and the interconnectedness of everything around us. Never have I felt myself so mentally stretched, spiritually expanded, and personally profoundly shaped by a book on science or theology."

Phyllis Infanzon

ANONYMOUS COMMENTS FROM

UNIVERSITY OF ST. THOMAS'

PROFESSOR EVALUATIONS

"This course is truly life changing. The possibilities of how faith & science interact are endless and as we know, we have only touched the surface of knowledge about this subject. I pray that people will become more open to this information, and that they will incorporate its teachings into their life."

≈≈≈≈≈≈≈≈≈≈≈≈≈≈≈

"One of my best courses so far! Dr Hesse book and presentations on Faith and Science has helped me to see further the integration of the human person with nature and divinity. From the micro to the macro all the universe is an expression of God's love. This class encouraged students to participate in open discussions about controversial topics from a non-judgmental approach. Open to dialogue is how we can learn from one another and the world."

≈≈≈≈≈≈≈≈≈≈≈≈≈≈≈

"For someone who has no science background, it sparked an interest, however with that said, I somewhat felt lost moving from one point to the other very quickly. I understand the mission in the movement of topics, but again, if you have no science background, it is overwhelming. Then to extract something to write a paper on was difficult and challenging, however, the class overall helped me process the point of the class. Dr. Hesse is an excellent teacher with very good science and faith backgrounds so this class is perfect for him and for the graduate studies program. Thank you, Dr./Deacon. Hesse."

≈≈≈≈≈≈≈≈≈≈≈≈≈≈

"Well prepared and well organized."

≈≈≈≈≈≈≈≈≈≈≈≈≈≈

"I heard a lot of honest sharing; I feel I am not alone on the journey."

≈≈≈≈≈≈≈≈≈≈≈≈≈≈

"This is a remarkable course, one that has given me much to think about and sparked deep personal and spiritual growth. Offering this course via ZOOM made it possible for several people to take the course who would not have been able to otherwise. I believe the course is extremely well suited for this format from beginning to end. Dr. Hesse is a gifted teacher, creative and responsive in his approach to delivering the course content and drawing students into discussion. I highly recommend this course."

CONTENTS

INTRODUCTION

This teacher's guide is based on the practical lessons learned from teaching Faith and Science (F&S) graduate courses for credit using my book *Faith and Science: A Journey into God's Mystical Love*[1] as the textbook. Courses were taught at the: Pontifical University Regina Apostolorum in Rome for its master's degree in F&S; University of St. Thomas in Houston for its master's degree in faith and culture; and Archdiocese of Galveston-Houston for ongoing education of Catholic clergy. The syllabus for those courses was used to develop this guide.

Students were asked to: read the textbook chapter for the next class; participate in class discussions; submit a 1 to 3 paragraph journal report after each class describing what was learned in that class and how it may affect the student's life; give three presentations at the end of the course; and pass the final exam. The presentations and final exam are described in the Assignment chapter of this guide.

Splitting the material into digestible pieces based on the time available can be a challenge. I dedicated two classes to each of the more scientific Chapters 3 to 6, each of which has three subchapters. I taught the first two subchapters in the first class and the last subchapter in the second class. This division allowed a summary discussion of the three subchapters during the second class.

OBJECTIVE

The course objective is to explore theistic faiths of how God reveals truth chronologically through nature, tradition, and scripture, showing self-consistency between the three. It is meant to have practical application in ministerial applications affirming God's unconditional love for us. The

---

[1] Hesse, Robert J. *Faith and Science: A Journey into God's Mystical Love*. (New York: Crossroad, 2022)

book's unusual genre, combining memoir and textbook, is meant to encourage students to personalize and integrate what they learn into their own belief system.

OVERVIEW

The course shows science affirms faith in the relational nature of God's unconditional indwelling love for everyone on earth. It covers the exponential, asymptotic convergence of faith and science from physics to creation, chemistry to life, biology to consciousness, and psychology to mysticism. It tracks the instructor's recently published textbook receiving international interest. It is accessible in language non-scientists and non-theologians can understand and includes numerous quotations from scripture, renowned scientists and theologians. It is interfaith in scope with a Catholic emphasis. It covers practical applications for many ministries with the support of numerous international conferences. It is inspired by St. Augustine of Hippo: *"Miracles are not contrary to nature, but only contrary to what we know about nature."*

ORGANIZATION

This guide is organized to follow the chapters of the book. Most chapters include sequentially: *objective, overview, outline, review, discussion,* and *reflection* described as follows:

CHAPTERS

1. *Objective* describes the purpose of the chapter.
2. *Overview* gives a summary of subject matter of the chapter.

CLASSES

The following are contained in one or two classes depending upon how many classes were required to cover the chapter.

3. *Outline* provides a table of contents of the sub-chapters.

4. *Review* covers the highlights of the previous class followed by any subjects my students struggled with. In addition to the material listed, the teacher is encouraged to include any subjects their students needed help with, based on previous class discussions and journals they were asked to submit after each class.

5. *Discussion* section includes ten questions designed to encourage open dialogue at the end of each class and ends with a key question to segue to the next class.

6. *Reflection* is meant to inspire the students to personalize their journal entries with what they learned during the class. These are written by my editor, Jan Masterson, who is uniquely qualified. As neither a theologian nor scientist, she is representative of most of the students and therefore gave valuable perspective. She edited the book, and we engaged in many spirited discussions, which led her to ultimately return to her Catholic faith after a 40-year absence.

1 - MOTIVATED TO LOVE

OBJECTIVE

The objective of this chapter is to encourage students to explore and identify their own hurts. To have them examine how those hurts may have affected their belief systems. This is meant to encourage them to personalize their learning process as the F&S course moves forward.

OVERVIEW

Discussions briefly cover the very personal nature of the motivations behind a journey away from and back to Catholicism through science, ultimately leading into God's mystical love. It is meant to help others on their journeys and in their ministries. We are all on a journey seeking God, but God actually finds us. This is inspired by theologian and mystic Meister Eckhart: *"God is at home, it's we who have gone out for a walk."*

OUTLINE

1. SECULARISM & SCIENCE: *I had all the answers* is an example of turning away from grounded faith beliefs and switching to a prideful approach to life.
2. RELINQUISHING CONTROL: *Letting go and letting God* is an example of facing our limitations and the first appearance of humility.
3. MYSTICISM TO LOVE: *God is relationship* is an example of the movement to trust in God's loving relationship.

DISCUSSION

1. Have you been hurt by the behavior of others?
2. Were you angry at the person's whole group?
3. Did it last a long time or only momentarily?
4. Who did anger hurt more, perpetrator or you?

5. Did you change your belief system due to the hurt?
6. Did your feelings affect your well-being?
7. Did your reaction affect your spiritual journey?
8. Did you evaluate why you felt the way you did?
9. Was there an AHA moment of enlightenment?
10. Did your perspective on life and death change?

If we don't know where we are going, do we need principles to guide us? Stay tuned for next class: Revelation to Principles

REFLECTION

Since I edited the book, attended classes, and feel reasonably confident I know its content, I was able to focus on listening with my head and my heart. I sought to ask thoughtful questions. I set aside my fear and accepted I needed to be brave enough to pose the question. When I made a comment, I tried to make sure it was clearly and humbly offered. I tried to always listen respectfully to the comments and questions of others. I am seeking to gain knowledge and grow spiritually from the lessons presented. I wonder if I will learn anything more since I edited the book through nine drafts. Time will answer that question.

2 - REVELATION TO PRINCIPLES

OBJECTIVE

The objective of this chapter is to enable scientists, non-scientists, theologians and non-theologians to better understand the assumptions and basic tenants of the subjects discussed and more easily communicate with the scientific secular world.

OVERVIEW

Discussions show God's revelation of the assumptions about and principles of faith and science used in this course, which shows science addresses the question "how?" and faith the question "why?" It includes: love, non-dualism, logic, methods, notations, constants, and definitions. This enables better understanding of course classes and better ministerial communication with the secular world of science and the spiritual world of religion. It is inspired by St. Pope John Paul II: *"Science can purify religion from error and superstition. Religion can purify science from...false absolutes."* And by Albert Einstein: *"Science without religion is lame, religion without science is blind."*

OUTLINE

1. GOD'S REVELATION: *God manifested in everything* is an explanation on the number of ways God reveals truth to us, though not all faiths share this belief.
2. FAITH PRINCIPLES: *Love others as God loves us* contains the faith assumptions used in the class, though not all faiths share these assumptions. The focus is on relationships between faith and reason, body and soul and God and man.

3. SCIENCE PRINCIPLES: *Always seek truth* is necessary for the student, particularly non-scientific students, to understand scientific terminology, deductive and inductive reasoning and the concepts and tools used in science.

REVIEW

This is an opportunity to summarize any common themes you observed among the personal stories shared in the previous class.

DISCUSSION

1. What are core Catholic and scientific principles?
2. Can we prove God's existence or non-existence?
3. Is our faith dualistic or non-dualistic?
4. Can faith and reason contradict each other?
5. What is a scientific theory?
6. How do we use deductive and inductive reasoning?
7. What three ways does God reveal Himself to us?
8. Does knowing life's "how" help with life's "why"?
9. Do faiths' principles differ and what is the result?
10. Are F&S asymptotically converging?

If we follow our principles, how do they affect our journey into discovering the universe and its beginning? Stay tuned for next class: Physics to Creation

REFLECTION

I am surprised the explanation of the science definitely stretched my brain. Didn't expect that. I hope during subsequent classes I am better prepared to grasp the scientific principles being discussed and not be so surprised I still don't understand many of the topics. If I am being challenged, I can only guess at what the students are thinking. I hope by the end of the course, I can put all of them together into an understandable whole. I have a clear, well-defined set of ethics by which I live. However, I am open to modifying or even abandoning something

I believe to be true; but I will need to be convinced by both logic and faith. I suspect this will be my greatest challenge as the course progresses.

3 – PHYSICS TO CREATION

OBJECTIVE

The objective of this class is to see God as Awe and to appreciate His preconceived plan to create life in us before He created the universe.

OVERVIEW

Discussions demonstrate God is Awe by the Anthropic Principle, which states God planned to create life in us even before creating the universe. It covers the relationships between: the universe's vast magnitude and Nicene Creed; stars birth-death and continuing creation; light and worship; dark energy-matter and scripture; Newton's gravity and love; Einstein's general-special relativity and the afterlife; Fr. Lemaitre's Big Bang Theory and creation; Einstein's unified theory and atoms of life; and wormholes and heaven. It is inspired by Colossians 1:16: *"For in him were all things created, in the heavens and upon the earth, things visible and things invisible . . . All things have been created through him, and unto him."*

FIRST CLASS

OUTLINE

1. UNIVERSE'S MAGNITUDE: *God is Awe* is meant to show the immense magnitude of the universe by pretending to use a telephoto lens on our planet earth. Then expanding to a wide-angle lens to view our solar system, other stars, and other galaxies. And finally, the vastly greater invisible dark matter and energy.

2. MATTER & ENERGY: *Jesus the Man energized us* discusses the attractive forces of Newton and God and man. It describes Einstein's curvature of the universe giving a fresh approach to eternity being

unrestrained by space and time. It ends with relativity theory and wormholes, which postulates the possibility of how God could communicate with us between the present to past and future events.

REVIEW

1. GOD'S REVELATION:
    Nature before Tradition or Scripture
2. FAITH PRINCIPLE:
    Love Others as Christ Loves Us
3. SCIENCE PRINCIPLE:
    Empiricism, Rationalism, and Skepticism
4. SPIRITUAL JOURNEY:
    Movement from Principles to Creation

Students often struggle with the Eastern and Western differences in the definitions of dualism and non-dualism. In this course we apply the Western definitions as follows.

Western is non-dualistic in claiming relationships, not on equivalence, but mutually meant for each other as applied broadly to God and man, body and soul, and faith and reason. Western non-dualism attributes include: relational existence, Universe partially knowable, free will exists, shared Oneness, God creates, contemplation is a gift.

Eastern philosophy applies the terms differently with the following attributes: more dualistic vis-à-vis reincarnation, equivalency in essence, universe is an illusion, inseparable existence, become One, mind creates, meditation is experiential.

DISCUSSION

1. Is God constrained by space and time?
2. What does "eternal life" really mean?
3. Does outside the universe have any meaning?
4. Are forces and love both relational and unitive?

5. Explain Einstein's mental Special Relativity experiment.
6. Explain the Equivalence Principle.
7. Is there an edge to the Universe?
8. Explain Einstein's General Theory of Relativity?
9. How is Moon in geosynchronous orbit?
10. What ministries can use what was covered?

Big Question: If the Universe is so big and mostly unseen, how did it come into existence? Stay tuned for the next class: The Big Bang

REFLECTION

I thought I understood the concept of time and space. While working on the book, I learned I had both all wrong. Even after reading the manuscript nine times and listening to Bob patiently explain the scientific definitions in class, I still have a problem grasping time and space don't exist as my human brain understands them. The only way I can think of these concepts is to accept they are man-made constructs we use to make some sort of sense of our world. I hope Bob isn't disappointed in my way of accepting these concepts, but at this time in my learning curve, it is the best I can do.

SECOND CLASS

OUTLINE

3. BIG BANG: *God's creative love is explosive* explains the expanding universe is a continuous act of God's creation. How the forces of nature are all at work in the beginning of the universe, the singularity at the Big Bang. Those forces were so well balanced, they led to the understanding God preplanned life at the very beginning.

REVIEW

1. UNIVERSE'S MAGNITUDE:
   Over a billion trillion stars which is only 4%

2. GENERAL RELATIVITY:

   Gravity is dimples in space

3. SPECIAL RELATIVITY:

   Space and time relative to each other

4. WORMHOLE THEORY:

   Space-time continuum folded and connected

DISCUSSION

1. What does the singularity tell us about God?
2. How long did creation take?
3. How do we see beyond the visible spectrum?
4. Who is the father of the Big Bang Theory?
5. What are the attributes of the singularity?
6. What sacred texts are applicable to creation?
7. How was life predetermined at singularity?
8. Are F&S changing from static to dynamic?
9. How can we see back in time?
10. What ministries can use what was covered?

Big Question: If within minutes of the Big Bang, atoms formed then stars, which emitted atoms currently in our bodies, how did DNA form? Stay tuned for the next class: Chemistry to Life

REFLECTION

I am in awe at the size of the universe. I am in awe of the Entity who is responsible for such an incredible creation. I am in awe I exist and God knew me at the Singularity. The more I learn about Him and what He created, the more I do not understand how some people do not believe in a Supreme Being who is responsible for all we see and hear and experience. Another example of my human brain struggling with understanding science and God's wonder. For me, both have become "unknowable." Question: Will I ever know either completely?

4 - CHEMISTRY TO LIFE

OBJECTIVE

The objective of this chapter is to show the evolutionary process of God's creation, all of life's oneness, of us as co- creators and God's continuing involvement in our future union with Him.

OVERVIEW

Discussions show the evolutionary process of God's creation, of life's oneness, us as co-creators, and God's continuing involvement in our future. It covers the relationships between: subatomic-atoms-molecules and the God particle; chaos theory and virtues-vices; quantum uncertainty and God's answer to prayers; non-local universe and God's universal presence; quantum entanglement and God's infinite availability; microbes-DNA-cells and the Body of Christ; and evolutionary theory and our ongoing co-creation. It is inspired by Jeremiah 1:5: *"Before I formed you in the womb, I knew you, before you were born, I dedicated you, a prophet to the nations I appointed you."*

FIRST CLASS

OUTLINE

1. SUBATOMIC TO ATOMS: *The smallest among us loves* shows the connection of subatomic particles to the singularity and the God particle. Shows the role uncertainty and chaos have in our inability to know nature and God. It ends with the non-local universe, God being everywhere.
2. DNA TO CELLS: *God imprints His love in us* as atoms build to molecules of life, amino acids, to primordial soup and the

development of DNA. It shows the analogy of DNA to the Body of Christ, common within all of life.

REVIEW

1. ANTHROPIC PRINCIPLE:
   Universe Specifically Created for Life
2. BIG BANG:
   In the First Few Minutes Came Atoms for Life
3. GENERAL & SPECIAL RELATIVITY:
   God not Constrained by Space and Time
4. STAR DUST:
   Source of Every Atom in Humans

DISCUSSION

1. Is God's creation ongoing and non-linear through evolution?
2. Are either nature or God totally knowable?
3. Can God intercede in creation and if so, via what indeterminacies?
4. Is DNA analogous to the Body of Christ?
5. Can God be non-locally everywhere?
6. Is DNA indicative of spiritual oneness?
7. Is there life on other planets and if so, would it be like us?
8. Can the Word be different flesh on different planets?
9. Do uncertainty and chaos affect your image of God and free will?
10. How could you use what you learned in loving ministry to others?

Big Question: How did a complex molecule like DNA develop into life?
Stay tuned for next class: Microbes to Humans

REFLECTION

I understand infinite means something goes on and on and on. I accept God is the only entity capable of this phenomenon. My quandary is how to measure the universe since we can't see all of it and can only guestimate its size using mathematical formulas. Perhaps because I am not a scientist and not particularly adept at math, the formula "thing" doesn't compute in my brain. I understand the words but it is a challenge to apply the information to the size of the universe.

SECOND CLASS

OUTLINE

3. MICROBES TO HUMANS: *God's ongoing creation* discusses the non-linear progression of evolution during the Cambrian Explosion and breakup of Pangea, the earth's original land mass, into continents. This section explains the often-misunderstood principles of evolutionary theory leading the migration of humans across the continents and to the development of the races.

REVIEW

1. UNCERTAINTY PRINCIPLE:
    God and Nature not completely knowable
2. CHAOS THEORY:
    Chaos not chaotic; potential for good
3. NON-LOCAL UNIVERSE:
    God and Information Instantly Everywhere
4. WORMHOLE ENTANGLEMENT:
    Communication Across Space-Time?

Students often struggle with the definitions of "infinite" and "nothing." Because these are critical words to understanding the course, even for the later chapters on mysticism, the following is offered as clarification.

INFINITE: Some think if they can't comprehend the vastness of say the universe, then it is infinite, which it is not. This is a common mistake. Infinite means unending, boundless. God is infinite. In mystical terms it means the Oneness of God. God is the unknowable infinite. We are called to embrace the unknowable, infinite God.

NOTHING: Most think "nothing" means "non-existent", which is the main dictionary definition. In this course we use the etymological definition meaning "no thing" that is not constrained by space and time. God is No-Thing. In mystical terms He is Nothing. God is the unknowable Nothing. We are called to embrace the unknowable Nothingness of God.

DISCUSSION

1. Is creation ongoing and non-linear evolution?
2. Are either nature or God totally knowable?
3. Can God intercede; via what indeterminacies?
4. Is DNA indicative of spiritual oneness?
5. Do uncertainty and chaos affect God's image?
6. What is the Cambrian Explosion?
7. What was the Pangea Supercontinent?
8. Did humans evolve from monkeys?
9. How is race migration measured?
10. What ministries can use what was covered?

Big Question: If all life shares almost completely the same DNA molecule, why didn't monkeys build skyscrapers and land on the moon? Stay tuned for next class: Biology to Consciousness

REFLECTION

I am convinced God has not given up on the world. I see creation in action every time I encounter a pregnant woman or any furred, finned or feathered creature giving birth. Every time a tree buds, a flower blooms, grass grows, I know God is at work. A simplistic acceptance of on-going creation, I know, but one I can understand and accept. God continues to create. I believe if God wants other planets populated, they must be. He is the Supreme Being so why should I question what He can do.

5 - BIOLOGY TO CONSCIOUSNESS

OBJECTIVE

The objective of this chapter is to understand the brain's complex functions and how they relate to bioethics, free will and soul. And to understand the extensive medical studies on the healing effects of faith, liturgy and prayer.

OVERVIEW

Discussions show the brain's complexity, its functions, and how they relate to life's daily spiritual challenges such as virtue, sin, forgiveness, gratitude, repentance, etc. It covers the relationships between: brain mapped functions and moral decisions; brain-universe networking and creation's oneness; sleep stages and scripture revelations; conscious-unconscious and prayer; faith-liturgy-prayer medical research and physical-spiritual healing; brain disorders and moral culpability; conscience-free will and bioethical non-judgementalism; and confirmation bias and original sin. It is inspired by Nobel Prize winning physicist for quantum theory, Max Planck: *"I regard consciousness as fundamental. I regard matter as derivative from consciousness. We cannot get behind consciousness. Everything that we talk about, everything that we regard as existing, postulates consciousness."* And by St. Augustine of Hippo: *"I cannot grasp all that I am."*

FIRST CLASS

OUTLINE

1. BRAIN & FUNCTIONS: *Seeing God dwelling within* is a discussion about the brain's functions by scans. It describes the analogies between the brain and the universe. It discusses the competing

dualities of the brain, especially the conscious and unconscious. How God can speak to us through the unconscious.

2. CONSCIENCE & FREE WILL: *Free choice to love* discusses how evolutionary theory cannot explain free will or conscience, yet brain disorders demonstrate they exist. Why and how faith must contribute via the concept of the informed conscience related to ethics and bioethics.

REVIEW

1. CAMBRIAN EXPLOSION:
      Evolution is non-linear
2. DISSIPATIVE STRUCTURES:
      Humans do not violate 2nd Law of Thermodynamics
3. EVOLUTIONARY THEORY:
      Humans did not Evolve from Apes
4. HUMANS' ARRIVAL:
      Latecomers in Evolution

DISCUSSION

1. Has science located conscience and free will?
2. Can we judge others' moral culpability?
3. How are civil and moral law different?
4. What about the soul makes us human?
5. Are subjective and objective sin different?
6. Does consciousness affect the meaning of "Genesis"?
7. Are the brain and universe related?
8. Do prejudices automatically mean sinfulness?
9. How can we unload unconscious to conscious?
10. What ministries can use what was covered?

If God and free will exist, what are the results of research on the subject? Stay tuned for next class: Healing Research

REFLECTION

I don't see a need to know where conscience and free will exist in the brain in order to understand and maybe modify my behavior. It is more important to know and accept they do exist. However, if I am studying the brain as a researcher, it is necessary to know the "where: in order to understand "how" the brain works. Knowing that fact is not going to help me grow emotionally or spiritually.

SECOND CLASS

OUTLINE

3. HEALING RESEARCH: *Divine Healer within* is a review of the extensive scientific research on the healing benefits of faith belief, regular church attendance and frequent prayer. Ending with the challenge of scientific evidence for confirmation bias, which leads logically to the next chapter.

REVIEW

1. BRAIN & UNIVERSE:
      Similar & Interdependent
2. CONSCIOUS & UNCONSCIOUS:
      Both Needed to be Fully Human
3. INFORMED CONSCIENCE:
      Can't Judge Others' Sins Inside Their Brain
4. SPIRITUAL JOURNEY:
      Movement from Consciousness to Biases

DISCUSSION

1. What is difference between healing and curing?
2. Are correlation and causality different?
3. Did and does Jesus heal non-dualistically?
4. Do theistic faith, liturgy, and prayer heal?

5. Does our image of God affect our healing?
6. Does forgiving = forgetting; God's justice = mercy?
7. Does a culture of death survive?
8. What are the two forms of prayer and is one better?
9. Is confirmation bias in the unconscious?
10. What ministries can use what was covered?

If our unconscious brain contains confirmation bias including prejudices, how can our free will overcome that? Stay tuned for next class: Psychology to Mysticism

REFLECTION

I sincerely believe prayer helps the healing process. Never gave much thought to how my image of God or that of the person for whom I was praying may have contributed to that belief. I "knew" it was my prayers that helped my beloved Gram feel better. When prayers for my husband were not answered as I hoped, I was forced to accept God knows best, not mortal me. Difficult, but valuable lesson.

The discussion of healing versus cure helped me understand there are all types of healing and curing. I was focused on the physical healing; rarely gave a thought to the spiritual aspect. This lesson gave me a new perspective to consider.

6 - PSYCHOLOGY TO MYSTICISM

OBJECTIVE

The objective of this chapter is to understand the interfaith commonality of contemplative prayer and its relationship to the altered states of consciousness of a mystical experience and Near-Death Experience (NDE). It describes how the unloading of the unconscious can allow for Divine healing. Understanding how the brain is trainable to help overcome sin and to better understand the three transcendent events of creation.

OVERVIEW

Discussions show how the brain is trainable to help overcome habitual sin, anger, grief, and other challenges of the human condition. It covers the relationships between: brain neuroplasticity and prayer; unloading confirmation bias and prayer; meditation-contemplation and spiritual-physical healing; altered states of consciousness and mystical experiences; NDE-mystical research and afterlife-ecstasy; neuroscience and neurotheology; singularity-mystical attributes and heaven; collective consciousness and God; wormhole entanglement and past-future knowledge; and God's oneness and evolutionary universal love. It concludes with *kataphatic* and *apophatic* prayer history, psychology, theology, methodology, and a practicum of contemplative prayer. It is inspired by theologian Fr. Karl Rahner: *"The devout Christian of the future will either be a 'mystic', one who has experienced something, or he [she] will cease to be anything at all"* and by Albert Einstein: *"…most beautiful emotion we can experience is the mystical."*

FIRST CLASS

OUTLINE

1. MEDITATION & CONTEMPLATION: *Indwelling God* is a discussion of the theology and history of meditation and contemplation, which are often misunderstood terms. Followed by the methodology of contemplative prayer and its dealings with thoughts. An understanding of how prayer can unload the unconscious and spiritually heal confirmation bias.

2. ALTERED CONSCIOUSNESS: *States of God's presence* describes mystical experiences and God's presence within, followed by a discussion of NDE. Both NDE and mystical unrelated to NDE are recognized as common transcendent events between this life and the next, which are comparable to the singularity at the Big Bang.

REVIEW

1. BODY & SPIRIT:
   Science Confirms Jesus' Non-Dualistic Healing
2. FORGIVENESS RESEARCH:
   Forgiver Heals More than Forgiven
3. BELIEF, LITURGY, & PRAYER HEAL:
   Science Confirms with Multiple Studies
4. CONFIRMATION BIAS:
   Science Shows We Tend to Misinterpret Data

DISCUSSION

1. Can we unload unconscious confirmation bias?
2. What is mysticism and contemplation?
3. Can anyone have a mystical experience?
4. Is human oneness due to the indwelling God?
5. What sacred texts confirm your mystical faith?
6. Are spirituality and religion mutually exclusive?
7. Is God the ultimate Universal Consciousness?

8. Is discursive or contemplative prayer better?
9. Can mystical and NDE both be Divine union?
10. What ministries can use what was covered?

How do meditation and contemplation affect our image of God? Stay tuned for next class: Neuroscience & Neurotheology

REFLECTION

I was introduced to the Universal Conscience in a psychology class many years ago. The concept helped me grasp why we just seem to "know" certain things. I lumped it together with cultural knowledge unconsciously passed from generation to generation. When Universal Conscious was combined with an Inner Spirit, my mind went into overdrive. Suddenly, science was crossing over into religion. Then the idea of the Inner Spirit being the third person of the Trinity was introduced. All of a sudden, I didn't know what to think. God in the person of the Holy Spirit dwells inside of unworthy me? No way! As people with a deeper spirituality than I started pointing out examples in my behavior, I was forced to accept, just maybe the idea wasn't ridiculous after all. I still struggle with Her inner presence, but I am slowly learning to rely on Her guidance and consult Her when I am in a quandary. I am still working on the impact of science and faith coming together. Mind bending!

SECOND CLASS

OUTLINE

3. NEUROSCIENCE & NEUROTHEOLOGY: *Earth and Heaven* discusses neuroscientific brain scans, which show prayer changes the brain because it has neuroplasticity. Neurotheology is doing research on states of saintly ecstasy. The experience of oneness reported by mystics is leading scientists to consider wormhole entanglement. It is God unconstrained by space and time in total union with us. This implies an image of God as the Universal Consciousness of love.

REVIEW

1. BODY & SOUL HEALED:
   Science Confirms Relational Healing
2. RELIGIOUS PRACTICE HEALS:
   Research: Faith, Liturgy and Prayer
3. FORGIVENESS HEALS:
   Forgiver Healed More Than Forgiven
4. SPIRITUAL JOURNEY:
   Movement from Biases to Love

DISCUSSION

1. Can science locate brain's free will & conscience?
2. Can God's image be Universal Unconsciousness?
3. Does God communicate through the unconscious?
4. Can we share in God's consciousness?
5. How can science study subjective experiences?
6. Does God communicate through synchronicity?
7. Can saints in the next life pray for us?
8. What are Divine attributes of NDE and SCE?
9. What are three examples of transcendent events?
10. What ministries can use what was covered?

If contemplative prayer changes our brain, how can it affect our spiritual journey? Stay tuned for next class: Called to Serve

REFLECTION

I believe in free will because I accept I am responsible for my actions and need to be prepared for the consequences. Never thought much about "where" free will and conscience is located in the brain. Same with conscious and unconscious. They just are.

Does God communicate with me? Sure does, if I am paying attention. Communication is a two-way proposition. To be heard, someone must be listening. Seems simple and straightforward to me. As I was listening to the spiritual and scientific explanation, these thoughts kept running through my mind: Does it really matter? Will I be a better person if I know the how and the why and the where? My Inner Being seems to be saying, "It matters if you learn to be more aware and pay closer attention to what God is telling you." So I continue to listen and learn.

7 – CALLED TO SERVE

OBJECTIVE

The objective of this chapter is to elicit reflection from students on the impact spiritual encounters may have had on them and what they were being called to do.

OVERVIEW

This chapter circles back to chapter one as a book end to my journey. It addresses how ultimately science and faith are calling us to serve as we see God dwelling within everyone. It gives the details of my mystical experience from rumination to ecstasy to recovery, which goes beyond words. It is a climax and convergence of my scientific and spiritual journey into God's mystical love. It is inspired by Luke 12:48b: *"…whoever wishes to be great among you shall be your servant; whoever wishes to be first among you shall be your slave."*

OUTLINE

RUMINATING THOUGHTS
   The Devil made me do it
LOVING ECSTASY
   God brings me home
RECOVERY & EVALUATION
   Love is what it's about

REVIEW

1. NEUROPLASTIC HEALING:
    Parkinson's, PTSD, Depression, Fear of Dying

2. ECSTASY PROPOSITION:
   Brain Wiring Proposition
3. WORMHOLE ENTANGLEMENT:
   Spanning Space and Time
4. COLLECTIVE ONENESS:
   Singularity, Mysticism, NDE

DISCUSSION

1. Are spiritual and religious mutually exclusive?
2. Has my image of God changed; if so how?
3. Where am I on my journey?
4. Do I more easily see God in others?
5. Am I less judgmental?
6. Have I had an NDE or mystical experience?
7. What are effects of God's universal indwelling?
8. Do many atheists exist by mis-defining God?
9. How is suffering and love salvific?
10. What ministries can use my experiences?

If prayer enables us to more easily see God dwelling within others, how can we better serve others? Stay tuned for next class: Epilogue on Service

REFLECTION

At one time, I was convinced I was spiritual but not religious. God has always been in my life. Institutional religion, not so much. Working on the book, I was forced to look into my heart and dig deep into my soul about what I was rebelling against. Was it religion or was it ignorant men? Gradually I came to understand I was rebelling because of confirmation bias: Blaming an entire institution for the failings of a few misguided men. Even though I have returned to the practice of my childhood church, I still struggle with the institution. And I still believe I am more spiritual than religious, although I am slowly coming to understand the two probably aren't mutually exclusive. Semantics?

Maybe. I like to think of myself as being honest. If I can't be honest with myself, and God, I am in big trouble.

EPILOGUE

OBJECTIVE

The objective of the Epilogue is to learn about the available F&S spiritual and intellectual resources and their applicable ministries.

OVERVIEW

Discussions show the resources available for faith and science, which can provide spiritual and intellectual support and opportunities. Numerous conferences are discussed, which include various combinations of the following topics: faith, science, medicine, religion, spirituality, prayer, consciousness, research, and interreligious dialogue. Based on the instructor's practical experience, numerous ministries are discussed, which benefit from science including: marriage preparation; Bible study; prison chaplaincy; hospital chaplaincy; liturgical services; preaching and homiletics; spiritual direction; youth and adult education; and seminary education. Discussions are inspired by Pope Francis: *"Dialogue between faith and science also belongs to the work of evangelization."*

OUTLINE

1. MINISTRIES & SEMINARIES: Includes example ministries in which the author has experienced the value of using F&S. Also includes the role of F&S in seminary curriculum.
2. CONFERENCES & RESEARCH: Includes the numerous F&S conferences categorized by their main mission, plus relevant F&S research.
3. INTERRELIGIOUS DIALOGUE: Includes discussion of the value of F&S in interfaith and interdenominational dialogue and shared ministries.

REVIEW

1. SPIRITUALITY & RELIGIOSITY:
    Do We Need Both for Relationships?
2. EFFECTS OF COURSE:
    Seeing God's Love and Presence in Others?
3. PERONALIZED COURSE:
    Did You Experience Personal Growth?
4. SPIRITUAL JOURNEY:
    How Will you Apply to Ministries?

DISCUSSION

1. How does being spiritual and religious help in ministries?
2. What are guidelines for interfaith dialogue?
3. What conferences are relative to your ministry?
4. What organizations apply to your ministry?
5. What is your favorite ministry?
6. Can you minister whether you are clergy or layperson?
7. What are effects of God's universal indwelling?
8. Do many atheists exist by mis-defining God?
9. Is your spiritual journey salvific to you and others?
10. What ministries can use what was covered?

REFLECTION

Even though I don't think of my activities as "ministries,' people I respect tell me they are. I maintain I am just being me.

I have been a columnist for thirty years. The content of my two columns is motivational in theme and intent. As Managing Editor of the CN newsletter, I correspond with four incarcerated men who offer helpful ideas for a life "inside the walls" column. I try to encourage them with upbeat letters subtly reminding them they are worthy of God's love. I have always offered warm hugs and loving smiles to everyone I encounter. Now I know I am sharing God's love. I don't know which ministries these activities fall into. What I do know is the Holy Spirit is guiding me so I joyfully accept my assignments.

ASSIGNMENTS

OBJECTIVE

The objective of the assignment of presentations is to give student's practical experience so they can confidently and effectively teach F&S to their students, who may not be theologians or scientists, theists or atheists.

OVERVIEW

Students are required to give three verbal presentations at the end of the course in the following order: *Book Reviews, Controversial Subjects, and Homiletic Sermons.*

In all presentations, the student picks the subject and gets preapproval from the instructor. The student submits to the instructor the digital presentation files in PowerPoint and/or Word as applicable. All presentations must be based on previous faith and science class content.

OUTLINE

1. *BOOK REVIEWS*: A 350–400-word, texted, single book review chosen from a short list of books provided by the instructor and taken from the textbook's bibliography.
2. *CONTROVERSIAL SUBJECTS*: A ten-minute PowerPoint presentation on a current controversial subject to a student-defined imaginary audience.
3. *HOMILETIC SERMONS* A six-minute texted homily based on a Sunday's scripture readings from any cycle A-C or from wisdom literature of the student's particular faith belief. Typically, a sermon can be on any subject, but a homily is on the readings of the day, which are common to all major Christian denominations. The purpose is to apply the readings to everyday life.

DISCUSSION

A brief, kind, and constructive critique after each presentation, is encouraged from the student audience with final summary by the instructor.

REFLECTION

One of the responsibilities of an editor is offering ideas for the author to consider. When I suggested Bob add keeping a journal to the class requirements, he was excited by the positive result. I know how much writing in a journal has helped on my journey, so I was sure it would help the students as they tried to integrate the new information into their daily life. He decided to make it an extra credit assignment. An excellent idea: Suggesting private introspection with no hidden agenda except to learn about themselves. An unexpected benefit for the instructor was insight into what further explanation students needed by first being a quiet observer of their spiritual journey.

EXAM

The courses I taught were graduate level, which led to the following instructions for the final exam. This is based on the philosophy the final exam is not meant to cause angst over memorization of minutia but is a continuation of the learning process. The principle for its construction was based on the necessity for the students to understand the most critical issues and conclusions of the course. The following were the instructions given to the students.

The final Faith and Science (F&S) exam will be take home and open book without in-person attendance. It will consist of essay explanations on your choice of topics from list below. Four essays are required from credit students and three from audit students. The seven available options provides flexibility for interfaith choices. Email essays to me no later than 9:30 pm, Wednesday, 10 May 2023, in Word format, not to exceed 400 words per topic.

1. Anthropic Principle and God
2. General and Special Relativity and heaven
3. DNA and Body of Christ
4. Confirmation Bias and Original Sin
5. Uncertainty Principle, Chaos Theory, and miracles
6. Wormhole Entanglement and mysticism
7. Singularity, NDE, SCE and heaven

This is meant to be a learning process so you can demonstrate your knowledge of the material and hone your skills in explaining the material to non-theologians and non-scientists. Each essay must contain the following with awe:

1. How scientists discovered the phenomenon.
2. How the discovery affected preexisting scientific understandings.
3. The scientific conclusions.
4. How conclusions affected faith, God's image, and example ministry.
5. Quotes from a scientist and theologian reinforcing F&S connection.

AUTHOR

Robert Hesse Ph.D. is a permanent Catholic deacon. He is Chairman and Co-founder of Contemplative Network, dedicated to teaching interfaith contemplative prayer, sponsoring scientific research on its healing effects, and establishing ministries based on the research. He was inspired by Trappist Monk, Fr. Thomas Merton, while on retreat at Gethsemani Trappist monastery. Later he was appointed by Trappist Fr. Thomas Keating, Commissioned Presenter of Contemplative Outreach Ltd. (COL) and Keating's emissary to the first COL dialogue with the Mind & Life Institute, in response to an invitation by The Dalai Lama to Keating. He is retired Vice Chairman and current faculty member of the interfaith Institute for Spirituality and Health, the oldest such organization in the U.S.A. located in the Texas Medical Center, the largest in the world. He is also Adjunct Professor at the University of St. Thomas and faculty member of the Magis Center and Emmaus Spirituality Center. He is instructor at the Pontifical University Rome, which grants a master's degree in F&S. He has given numerous international and interfaith presentations, retreats and courses on contemplative prayer and F&S, having degrees in both.

Contemplative Network: www.contemplative.net

Presentations: www.youtube.com/ContemplativeNetwork

Robert Hesse is available for interviews, presentations and seminars. Contact him at rjh@contemplative.net with a copy to editor@contemplative.net.

EDITOR

Jan Masterson is Director Communications for Contemplative Network. She has edited books on faith and science, travel adventures, faith and culture, slide presentations, and numerous articles, reports and research papers. She has interviewed prominent people and people on the street for profile and feature stories.

Jan is the Features Editor and writes a quarterly column, *The Garrulous Grandma,* for the *Eagle Vista*, a community newsletter with a readership of over 1,000. She is the Managing Editor of *Contemplative Network News & Views*, which has an international audience. During her limited free time, she facilitates a memoir-writing group, and is writing reflections for a daybook and essays for the second volume of her memoir.

Jan taught Continuing Christian Education classes and facilitated adult Sunday school discussions. As the daughter of an ecumenical family, for years she has studied faith traditions and Eastern and Western philosophies.

All issues of the CN newsletter, *Contemplative Network News and Views* are archived under *Resources* on the following web site:

Contemplative Network: www.contemplative.net

Contact her at editor@contemplative.net.